AMORE

DR. KAVYA V S

BookLeaf
Publishing
India | USA | UK

Presentation by *BookLeaf Publishing*

Web: www.bookleafpub.com

E-mail: info@bookleafpub.com

ISBN: 9789358311099

First edition 2024

DEDICATION

Dedicating a bunch of mixed darkness, lightness, laughter, hurting, healing and moreover a stretch of everything that goes by me in reel and real life.

Anything and everything is truly inspiring, be it the little things, the turns and twists, or the life altering events.

I haven't truly figured out who has stood by me and who hasn't, had a lot of people encouraging and discouraging, criticizing, and some who found inspiration from whatever I wrote.

I wouldn't mention the cliche of saying the two pillars in my life are my parents and of course my family, but yes they have had it tough understanding my trail of thoughts, because well that's the way it is with our brewed generation. And especially would like to dedicate to my sweetheart, my niece, my happiness package, ISHIKA. Welcome to the world dear it surely isn't what you think, but you will always find a fun aunt Phoebe in me and the emotional Ross in my poems, and a sarcastic Chandler in my comments, a lover Rachel in my well love life, an OCD mother Monica in my parenthood, a funtastic Joey in my friendship.

ACKNOWLEDGEMENT

Extremely grateful to my parents for supporting me in all my endeavors. Family is and always will be a constant in my life.

And extremely grateful to the few who always stood by me and pushed me forward to breach all my extents. There have been a handful of people in my life whom I will always keep close to my heart and close to my life. They will always be present in the movie called my life. And also acknowledging the few who have crossed the chapters in my life.

PREFACE

"Let the hearts be healed"
"Let happiness be the utmost priority"
"Let your wings unfold"

STATEMENTS

Why was I embarrassed and humiliated for my
sleep cycle?
Why am I judged for my survival?
Why was I silenced against a hand raised?
When thrown to the judgment was my
individuality?
Why was I named arrogance?
When I spoke about my preference.
Why did I need a hiatus for my mental health?
When I was driven by words to thoughts of
death.
Why did I lose sleep at night?
Driving it away with coffee and lights.
Why was I refused opinions?
When I had a past with torturers and villains.

Why wasn't I a priority?
When we were already the society's majority.
Why do I have to write my freedom words?
When we are caged like birds.
Why am I still afraid?
When my dreams and hopes are betrayed.
Why do I love depression?
When you have answers to my suppressions.
Why am I questioned?
When my answers are forever oppressed.

PRIDE

They were born Violet,
With rainbows on their wrists,
All night, all day they commit,
To love, the world still conflicts.
They are Indigo,
Wanting to kiss under the mistletoe,
But hid themselves in a condo,
Because the world watches through their
window.
They were colored Blue,
By phobians who drew,
Painting them like flu,
Never letting them through.
Amidst they kept their signals Green,
With their love to be seen,
Pure and raw with no screen,
Addictive like nicotine.

They swam in the Yellow,
Love stronger in the hollow,
Walking past the disgusted fellow,
Fears covered by the pillow.
They try to blend in the Orange,
Holding each other through the change,
Coming out bringing the grudge,
And even when close ones cringe.
But they shine the brightest in Red,
Proving their love isn't a weak thread,
Kicking judgments in repulsive head,
And together they lead.
Coz they are the Rainbow,
Who lets their love glow,
Amidst the dirt world throw,
Through the rough cold nights together they
tiptoe.

PAVE TO PERSONA

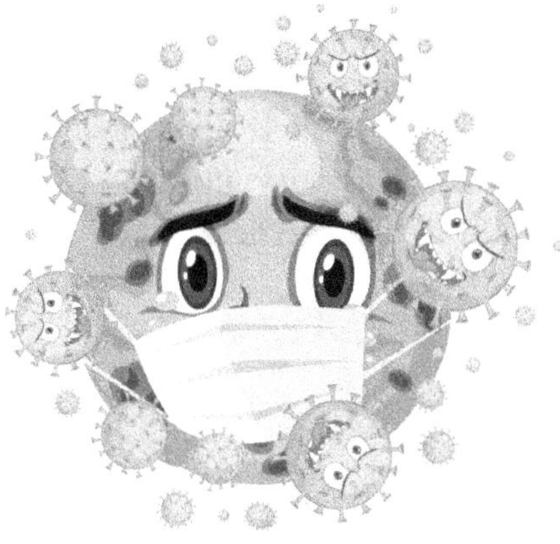

Along came Corona,
Bringing busy lives to a freeze,
Changing everyone's persona.
And all in one day,
Cooking became the new bae,
Art and cultures have a comeback,
While networks gave up in a sack.
Minimalism and DIY paved in,
Spending days with hands on the chin,
From lighting lamps and clapping hands,
Travel and shopping had a ban.
Washing hands and cleaning rooms,
Boys did learn to use the brooms,
Free Netflix and work from home,
The helpless and sick were given dorms.

When lockdown extended,
Singers, dancers and tiktokers accented,
Thoughts became dull and days became boring,
But united everyone was daring.
We fought back
Doctors, nurses and policemen as a pack.
Fallen will be the virus in defeat,
And we will see the glorious sight,
While dark fades,
Raindrops leaving dews.

STARTS

For a starter, I was living an idea,
For a reality check, it was just an exurbia.
The insanity I lived in was you,
Funny enough I should have seen the cue.
Burned down by the unphased beings,
I was drowned in your drawings.
I took my bags for a forever,
I ended up needing to recover.
Ever wondered how I write about the dark,
It's cause you put our story to an endmark.
I am happily pretending the happiness,
Covering up my foolishness.
Confused as fish would be an understatement,
Sorry not sorry about the achievement.

Bring me down all you want,
I would pass you off as silent.
I am out to ride the waves with the one,
While you can watch my shadows at dawn.
The pretence needs an end,
Cos the world is not that innocent.
Now you are confused,
Making you figure out the one would make me
amused.
Maybe that's the loop we live in,
Where you and I are separated by a screen.
I know where I started,
And the end is not with my beloved.

MINE

Tracing the fine lines,
Giving into your whines,
Cos at the end of the day,
You are Mine.
Pull me closer to your face,
Let me love the no space,
There's nothing about you I can't fall for,
You glued my heart the world tore.
We are a different kind of dream,
Days open to your smiles that beam,
True love ours in the wrong world,
Judging eyes make us whirled.
Far away I envy the hands on you,
That are just mine to,
Ruin me with your love,
Hands on your curve,
Cos at the end of the day,
You are Mine.

LOCK AND KEY

Smiles and the paths we crossed,
For you I came dressed,
Gave away glances to let you know,
You made me sway so slow.
I was just another one,
I realized and I run,
To the farthest end,
Forced myself to pretend.
That you don't break me,
The unrequited made me weak in the knee.
Unbelieve the looks in your eye,
Forget the future with your lie,
You will never catch me stare,
Cos it's only fair,
To let you have your voice,
Even if I let go of my choice.

I locked you in my heart,
With you as my key and my art.
Now I look away forming scars,
Burning pain away with cigars,
I can see the plea,
To a future we will never see,
Love that will never glee,
Neverland holding the lock and key.

CHORD C

The chaos is breaking me,
Little by little pulled apart,
Count one, two, three,
Let's paint my pain in art.
World gave me a trauma maze,
I am still running towards,
Wondering why I am still in their games,
Singing and dancing to their chords.
Giving up feels easy,
Happiness is now a survival,
Click me when I smile and freeze me,
Cos breaking me will be just a denial.

World who teaches and preaches should know,
Artists and rapists don't ring the same,
The similar -ist is not to blame,
It's your vision of truth that's not a white snow.

AN ALLURING SPECTRA

She isn't just a photography skill,
A lot more to her besides the still,
She hides her tears and fears in immaturity,
Now being worthy of someone's priority.
She found love so pure and true,
His hold on her hand grew so sure,
The big smile and so kind,
It was oh-so alluring to the mind.

DEEP DIP

This wasn't an option I chose,
It was the only choice I had,
I have lived in the chaos,
trying to run in the wild.
Screaming in colors,
Stuck like petals of flowers,
An ocean of joy I always have,
Yet solitude crept its way to pave.
The storm swept away rays of dreams,
Fear shaking to kick and scream,
And like drops of rain,
To the leaves I hung,
crying to never break the chain,
dewdrops forming the song I sang.

PITCH BLACK

Back against the cold wall,
Holding back the tears from falling,
Cos all I craved was pitch black.
Days and nights went by mono,
Red eyes and voice baritone,
Cos all I craved was pitch black.
Hiding and lying 24/7,
Drained dreams of heaven,
Cos all I craved was pitch black.
Hiding from pitty gazes,
Sarcasm cloaked empathy stays,
Cos all I craved was pitch black.

Standing on a cliff wanting the pain to end,
Calls dodged and steer clear from friends,
Cos all I craved was pitch black.
Voice stuck in the throat,
Pain clogged in heart,
Cos all I craved was pitch black.
Nights sleepless in loud cries,
Pillows soaked in tears,
Cos all I craved was pitch black.
Minutes, hours, days, months, years,
Closer to reality painted my black canvas in
fears,
Cos all I craved was pitch black.
Disfavored by fate,
Tranced by self-hate,
Cos all I craved was pitch black.

LOOP

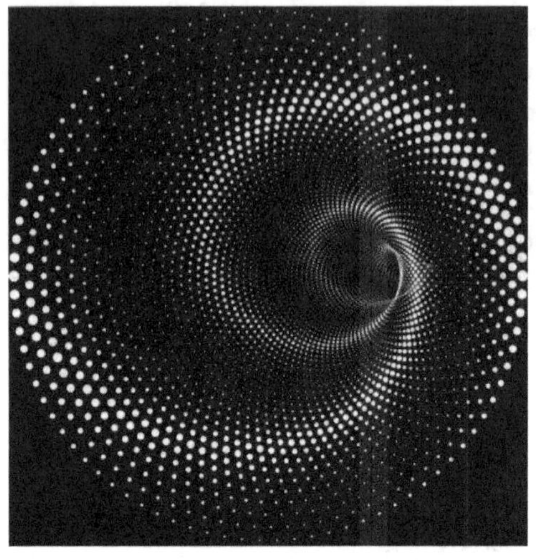

I stare into the dark night,
Screaming in black, no starlight.
No trace of sleep reaches out to me,
Teary eyes, nothing to see.
Shutting my thoughts,
Whimpers in the throat, feelings caught.
Soundless cries over days,
Dreams then built, now paused.
You the nameless call me,
Voice that let the silence of night flee.
Your words like a raindrop,
Drench me with laughter nonstop.
Soon the call ended,
I call out to the sleep promised.

But I can only lay empty,
Sleep far from reality.
Mornings come with head throbbing,
Faking smiles over last night's sobbing.
Grabbing my coffee cos I am a fool,
Wanting sleepless nights on loop to overrule.

FOREVER TOGETHER

I don't remember the day when my cries became
a joy to you,
But I do remember when you cried for my joy.
I don't remember when my first words made you
smile,
But I do remember your smile that became my
words.
I don't remember when you held my hands to
make me walk,
But I do remember every step that I held onto
your hands.
I don't remember when you helped me learn,
But I do remember your help made my lessons.
Thank you forever,
With you together.

A CALL

The many sleepless nights,
The many muffled cries,
The many fake smiles,
The many confused thoughts,
The many missing bruises,
And a few breaths.... It was just a call away,
And that was it...just that,
A whispered Hello,
Went on for hours,
To the days we broke,
The days we hated every cell,
To find new beginnings,
Forget the old broken ends,
And again a few breaths away...It was just a call
away.

DREAMING IN LOVE

We lay, lay, lay,
You by my side hey, hey, hey.
Oh baby, your breaths my music,
Serenading my heart cos I'm lovesick.
Your gaze screaming love shower,
Painting my dullness you cover, cover, cover.
Oh baby, hold me tight, tight, tight,
Never let you off my sight, sight, sight.
This love heavy,
Never let you go baby.
Cos the world out there's scary,
Let us never fall lonely.

DECEIVED

Why are my eyes dry?
Why can I not cry?
It is all very scary that I cannot let go,
Cannot get my feelings under the shadow.
You made me marshmallow,
Too soft to hurt put me out as shallow.
I am too drunk in pain,
Can you tell me how I ended up this vain?
Time passed,
And you let me when you weren't amused.
Playing dumb hurts me,
Meeting my eyes in the mirror reminds me of
my plea.
The games you pulled broke me bad,
Couldn't get that outta my head.
You were not one of my choices,
You were my first and last phases.
I amused in your sufferings,
Made me feel we are together losing.

Oh the lies you used,
To forget I wasted all night boozed.
I will learn to walk past you,
Cos you don't serve my favorite view.
And maybe I will get closure my friend,
Cos I have got a heart to mend.

POISON

Kiss me goodbye,
The last of your reply,
Don't look me in the eye,
When you can't stop the cry,
You are my only poison.
Where is the destiny we saw?
Oh was it for fate to redraw?
Was our love just a flaw?
Didn't our love lock like a claw?
You are my only poison.
You want me to explore,
Return me to before,
Sucking me out of love so raw,
Life without you taking over so slow,
You are my only poison.

We were so different but fit the puzzle,
Figuring crooks in your neck I nuzzle,
Your breath on my lips we frizzle,
your warmth cut the cold like a chisel,
You are my only poison.
Pretending I don't know you, we faking,
Did it ever work for we portray our longing,
Breaking our facade a million times cos we were
hurting,
We ready to let go but we aching,
You are my only poison.
Dreaming of you even when awake,
Letting go of my deepest love for your sake,
Though life without you I go psych,
Maybe our story remains a song so fake,
You are my only poison.

SHAME

Hefty, sticky, shorty, fatty, the name calls on the roll,
Made us crawl deep into a hole.
Laughter and fun all around,
Sacrifice ourselves for them to hound.
Why did we let them?
When we wanted to condemn.
Years around stress builds up,
To fats and sugars we let us slurp.
When everyone has the laughs with shaming,
Nobody saw the forthcoming.
Suicides, depressions took the poll,
While the laughing stocks had no soul.

Take heart-wrenching time to get out,
Crowd always making them doubt.
Had you been in their shoe,
Would you still have the same view?

FORBIDDEN

Is it all over?
Reality vanishing just like that?
Are nights just colder?
Will we abandon midchat?
Promises we made and broke,
But it was ours to figure and mend,
Memories we made and wrecked,
Now only silence is left to send.
We were two,
Why was one forbidden,
Was our story untrue,
Or were we so stubborn?
Weekends of fights grew for years,
Spites of misunderstanding grew,
Unforgivable were my tears,
Dreams of karma and revenge I drew.

Frustrated by my thoughts,
Solitude was the path I chose,
Hitting rock bottom of all sorts,
Pain drawn all over my bruise.

DESIRE

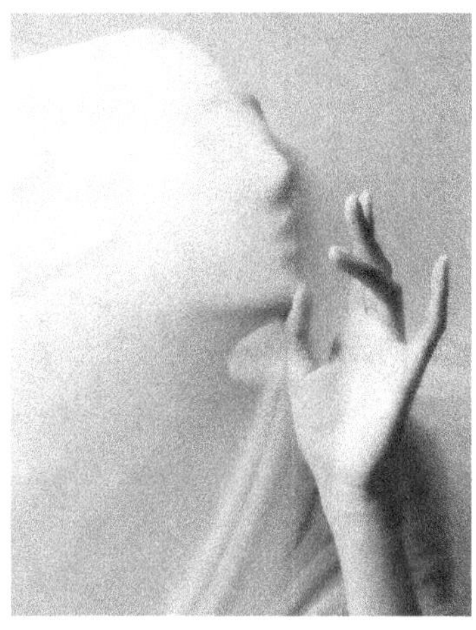

Your love drove me borders,
Did not see the unlove being harder,
Besotted were we in each other,
To see the bliss getting shorter.
Found no antidote to your emptiness,
Leaving me in this craziness,
My dreams keep getting lifeless,
I don't trust the brightness.
Wishing I had you back with desire,
The day you had me in Sapphire,
Moments we were caught in picture,
When your eyes held me in capture.
Don't wanna let go of the rhythms of night,
Now reliving the ecstasies of sight,
We were drunk on the height,
Why are we left with our lives to fight?

VOICE

Take me away, fly me far,
Talk to me no more.
Don't look me in the eye,
With love that can only lie.
Tired of the same sight,
Thoughts that only fight.
Not so sure, what do I do?
Get me away from the feels of blue.
Blur my visions of you,
Get a hold of the new.

STAR STRUCK

Round and round we will travel,
Ventures ending in destiny,
Struck in moments so heavenly,
Loops still left to unravel.
Vibes clicking all the way,
Capturing laughs in slow-mo,
Rays of light in the gray,
Laughter filling the hollow.
Heights of happiness,
Bounded by endless love,
No more cries of emptiness,
Drops of heaven under mazel tov.

GREED

You want the riches,
Live in a luxury,
I be the bitches,
Live inna suffering.
You took the road to heaven,
Dreaming the whites,
My dreams of tomorrow frozen,
Reality today bites.
Pretty lies to the loved,
You went too far,
While I was being shoved,
Truths burning scars.
You hide and hide and hide,
But you be leaving loopholes,
I watch you from the dark side,
Seeing you break into shambles.
Do I keep silent?
Do I save you?

POOLSIDE

Driven by humanity,

I'm lovin the insanity.

Splashing around the poolside,

Never smiled so wide.

Pen, papers and thoughts on life,

Thorns and flowers pathways to thrive.

Drunken wine talks,

Together intertwined walks.

Mind clouded,

Eyes bounded.

Hoping time doesn't lapse,

High on music we dance.

Group of madness,

Rejoicing in happiness.

REPEPEAT

Mild dews, music, memoir,
Yet again another au revoir.
Scribbles, sweets, sorry's,
Feeling numb and no worries.
Dance, drinks, drugs,
My newfound hugs.
Happy, hellos, hashtags,
Free from all red flags.
Love, laughter, life,
Looping my madness to thrive.

IDOL

She was the inspo,
Young, old and mid like to imit.
Fair, curvy, cute,
A combo to everyone's jelly.
He was the Romeo,
Loved in real and fantasy.
Cute, handsome, flawless,
Too hot to handle like they say.
Reels, vlogs fill insta walls,
Bounded by smiles and laughs,
Everyone's idol and star,
Was it always this shiny?
Behind the fame halls,
Fear and cries through walls.
Did the idol lose humanity,
Or was the expectation insanity?

Flashes and lights day and night,
Reels and reals left and right.
Too less to breathe,
Love behind the sheath.
Far away in dreams they held,
Reality bites let them bleed.

ABYSS

Drive me to the dark abyss,
I'm not calling it quits.
Push me off the cliff,
Not giving a damn to what if.
Born the survivor,
Burn me down, I'll fly through fire.
Dancing with the troubles,
Figure out the crazy puzzles.
Write me up, shut me down,
Watch me in a crown.
Undefined, undefeated,
Take a chair and be seated.
For you will see my rise,
To heights beyond the skies.

GRAY MAN

Zoning out amidst noise of crowd
Scrutinized, judged was his silence
Grey was what the world painted him
Yet colorful was his thoughts
Solitude never deemed him sadness
Intentional was his flaws
A ray of hope gleaming his eyes
Church bells spin his head around
Breaking his symmetry
Was it longing or waiting
The voice drops when asked
Lets him be in his dream
Winning the destruction of his soul

The world meets the ruin of him
4 o'clock was his time
The sleepless tormented dreamers
The time of fall
Save him catch him
From delicate shadows on his paths
From shame crippling him
Free from dwelling in the agony of unloved
Pave way for a wanderer
For his story ends in auf wiedersehen.

PROMISE

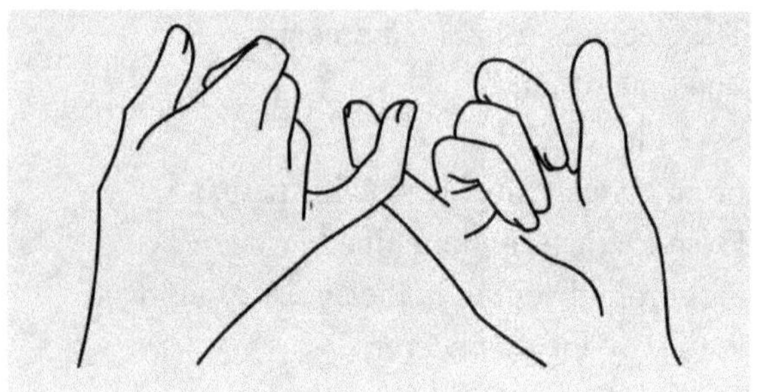

Promised me happiness,
Where was it when my tears were covered in
blurriness?
Promised me strength,
Why was I alone and tramped?
Promised me truths,
Where was it when I was smeared in loathes?
Promised me heaven,
Why was I meeting the dead end?
Promised me laughs,
Why was it all in photographs?
Promised a forever together,
Where do I find you in the heather?

DEADLY SINS

They be the sloths,
While making rules to show diligence.
They live as the ignorant pride,
While preaching on humanity.
They fight to fill their greed,
While judging others for their charity.
They rip apart the innocents for lust,
While crucifying others for their endless love
Their eyes gleaming in envy,
While throwing disrespect to others' gratitude.
They stuff with gluttony,
While screaming at others' temperance.
They throw wraths at intervals,
While destroying others' peace and patience.
Let the sins die,
Let the virtue live.

COLORS

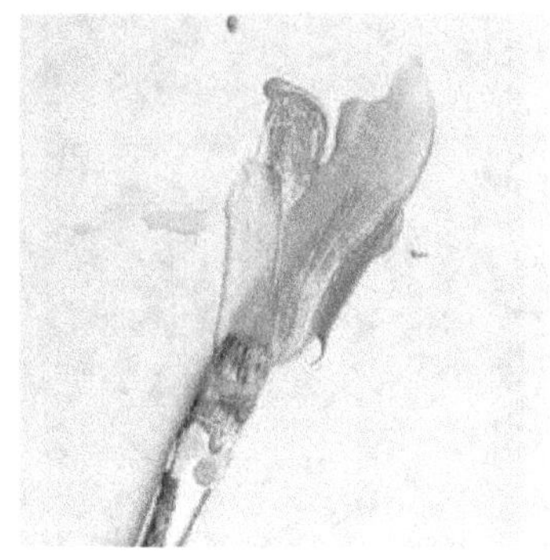

Dark alley, street light,
Eyes fluttered, love at first sight.
Forbidden heart, black canvas,
You are my color, my only bias.
Big screen, hidden moments,
Lovers at night, always my constant.
Ripped jeans, fearless,
Hold me closer, kiss in the abyss.
Rumors and rules to live,
Your hug is my wine dive.
Not a fairy tale, just struggles,
Our no space still tingles.
Duet songs, everyone's dreams,
They still throw insults in screams.
Your love is my dance to defend,
Baseless opinions, rumors behind.
This is us, our movie,
Breakthrough, let's go with our groovy.

STRINGS FROM NEVERLAND...

The music of goodbyes from the hearts,
One with a guitar, strings not attached,
Broken was his music, yet resonated with my
heartbeats.
One with a song, dreams of never forever,
Painful were his lyrics, yet swirled my feelings
at every sight.
One with the background music, words
unspoken,
Silence was his communication, yet erupted
cheers in my heart.
The one with the chorus, lost amidst the crowd,
Faceless was his love, yet spiked my soul to
him,
The One String from Neverland.

GAME OVER...

I will let you let you play,
Mock you to think you can slay,
Walk all over me like you own,
Diss me when you take the stone.
Bitches don't last in my world,
Stitches don't sew the broken wound,
Revenge is my gameplay,
Plunge into my new karma.
Told me I don't have a future,
Condescending me through your rumor,
Your name is big and famous,
Fear is where I meet your end though.

Laughing is my endcheer,
When I see your end in reverse gear,
Still resonates your words of deceivement,
April is when you pay my checks.
Don't cry now cause it's so sad,
To see your defeat so bad,
Does my spotlight scare you,
Drugs and clubs should be your warehouse.
Get away and far from my win,
Memoirs should revoke your begin,
Gameover for your crude plays,
Power hung on my walls forever.

SHINE...

Shine, shine, shine through the future,
Let your smiles weave your suture,
Grateful for the hearts,
Beating even when the year parts.
Helping hands, helpless minds,
Let love fill the blinds.
Tighter, higher through whenever,
Bonds and hearts forever.
Numbers and time don't decide,
Dimensions of life are just solitude.
Stronger, happier crossing the tide,
Blue, brighter, beauty is my triad.

NIGHTMARES....

There was just me and me,
The voices in me go free,
Heartbeats loudly plea,
Take me away from my screams.
Hands don't reach out,
Helpless agony doesn't shout,
Carved in graphy all my doubt,
All out there and unseen.
Eyes don't shed tears,
Soul creeps in fears
Nerves don't calm in beers,
Running in parallels forever.
World wakes in upbeat,
I close my eyes with torment in repeat,
Fake Smiles are my cheat,
To take away the momentum of pain.

Does the end have a light,
Neither dreams nor reality can fight,
No cuts, no wounds in sight,
How do I save the soul who is lone.
Where are the reasons,
Why are there no answers for seasons,
Are truths the real weapons,
Alas where to pierce in the midst of broken
shards.
I have come to me night after cries,
Calmed me on several tries,
Answers just in sighs,
Settling cold under the covers,
Feels secure under showers,
I am the answer to all inks in black.

COMMERCIAL…

Branded her name,
Launched her on the market,
Sold her passions for no shame,
Hiding the smashes of her racket.
Shy and coy was the girl in line,
Waiting for the gentle and bold guy,
Told she dances classical so divine,
Denied dreams of hers under the white sky.
Pick her up pick her up,
While her cries to soar high evicted,
Planning processions in club,
Celebrations and friendships are restricted.

Thou shall find her a warrior,
And leave her in dismal,
Society throws all kinds of slur,
Locking her in the secret chamber.
She shall see no light and day,
As proven to be committed a sin,
No man wants the pay,
To where he can't lead in.
That's the commercial,
Of the girl turning 21,
Brought up in denial,
Marriage is just another marathon.

RED THAT ONE DAY…

Red of flame that flickered,
That one day in the lanes,
Came out for cigars,
Blowing smokes into the blizzard.
Eyes don't meet in purpose,
Looking at sidewalks for reasons,
That one day in the cold season,
Breathless was I on your terrace.
Ignited fire on ice,
Passionate kisses fill the nights,
Stranger to stranger in paradise,
Smile caressing her lips, she writes.
That one day, that one red,
Etched on sleeves,
The next day we fled,
With our desire like thieves.

PSYCHO…

He was a rage,
Splashed by power,
Tallest yet in the front,
Success shining the brightest on him.
His fame in spotlight,
Looks on canvas and display,
For he was cool and handsome.
Was he all that?
Mysterious silence when asked,
Where was he on the 11th,
Aura demeaning the question put forth,
His musical laughter filled an answer.

Shiny blue was he in the film,
Water deep was his secrets,
Tides and waves of his acts,
Dig deeper into the shore of secrets.
Coffee was his day,
Black was his night,
Pure was his smile,
Psycho was his mind.

BESTIE…

Applications to friendship,
Vibes clicking, funny and cranky,
Secrets hold together,
But trust no one.
Pictures are good,
Memories are savory,
Travelling fills the weekend,
But trust no one.
The good character,
The priceless behavior,
Sweet as sugar they seem,
But trust no one.
Expectations are everyone's cup of tea,
For they want you for more,
Lies fill their good soul,
So trust no one.

WHITE COAT….

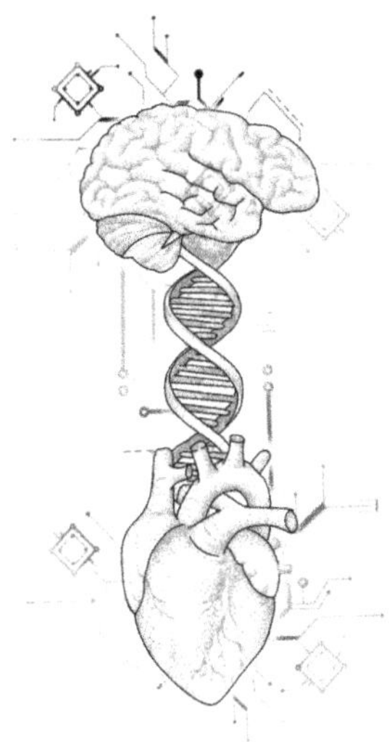

The white coats,
Work to life it knots.
Writeups and submissions,
Treating and preventing infections.
Easy to read and leave,
Harder than it seems to slave.
Google treats the curious mind,
Treating the souls are the ones behind.
Bloodless fields of surgery,
Skillful would be the mastery.
Five years of toil,
Knowledge brimming on boil.
Gold and silvers of marathon,
Game always being the walk on thorn.

Oblivious are people to the hardships,
Slurs and abuse thrown at the workshifts.
Rumors and gossips in the air,
Spread even by those in power.
Corruptions common in every field,
Present at every corner with an iron shield.
Heals the mind and soul,
Curing the body and saving with a logroll.
Prevent the sickness and stop the troll,
For it takes every cell,
To give up on oneself and be there for all.

RUNNING THE EXTRA MILE…

Dumbells and not taco bells,
Greens are the new leans,
Crunches and restrict the munches,
Proteins now fit the jeans.
Treadmills and not grills,
Water is the healthy order,
Stretches more and no more fudges,
Fiber is the new prescriber.
Fries, burgers, cola,
It's all so voila,
Spinach, eggs and boiled veggies,
To get the body everyone's all jellies.

Truth is harsh and bitter,
Health and diet are not gold that glitter.
Curvy is my body,
Flat is just my tv screen,
Sweets are my happy pills,
Carbs on which I spend the bills.
Dance is my sweats,
Fats even get outlets.
Love yourself, love your shapes,
Love your apples, love your frappes,
Love your walks, love your hoola hoops,
Love your broccolis, love your cake pops.
To please others, never dislike oneself,
The others spend concealing their imperfections,
Finding solace in others' insecurity, treating themselves,
Never be the food to quench others, be the diversions,
That they can never catch up even if they run that extra mile.

Y.O.U…

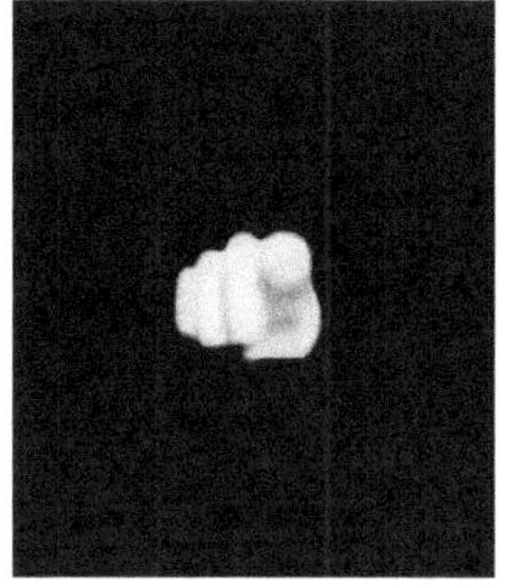

Do you see that?
The one that stops you on the street,
The one your teen admires.
Do you admire that?
The one everyone saves on screen,
The one even your girl aspires.
Do you know her?
The one who embodies perfection,
The one who takes every spot.
You see, admire and know her…
It's you and only you,
Just another reflected you,
You Own You.

SECOND LOVE…

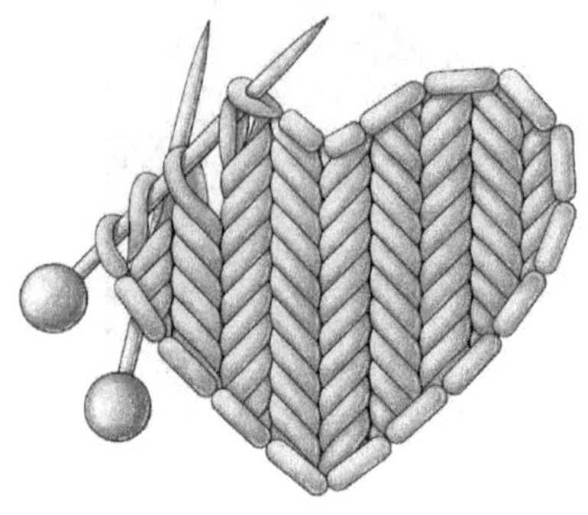

Corridors our honored valiant,
Basements our innocent witness,
Playgrounds our constant testaments,
Classrooms our cozy hideout,
Backseats our secret messenger,
Music our driven desire,
Sidewalks our concealed romance,
Second love our encounter,
Bencher not for any commoner.

WRITER…

I am your writer,
I pen your showdown,
All the amour now so bitter,
I see your frown,
Walking down the runway,
Threw in a glance at you,
Only to laugh at your delay.
Saw you lost the pride you grew,
I cast you in the book,
Made your empire shook,
Names changed, places changed,
You remained but a degrade,
This is my weapon,
Story is our unknown union,
Look out my lover,
Words of fire raise your shiver,
Painting you broken,
For all the art you have drawn.

FIRST…

Parting ways, senses chased,
Exhales and tingles decoded,
Yearnings raised,
Clumsy loitering fingers caressed,
Coarse voice, teary eyes,
Parading fear and excitement,
Half stranded on arms and scents,
The terrace witness the uneasy souls,
Straddling the chained melody,
Lips hover the desperate eternity,
Starry nights where thoughts kneeled,
Birthing the first kiss.

DECEMBER....

Coldest of all, my black sun,
Lets the night stall, lets me run,
I am called Amber,
Wandering every December,
Searching for a blue light,
Darkness gasp when I stroll through the night,
My breaths cut deep into the forbidden answers,
I am the child of moon,
Dreams and stars my constellation,
I am my mystery Amber on a warry December.

CAPTIVE…

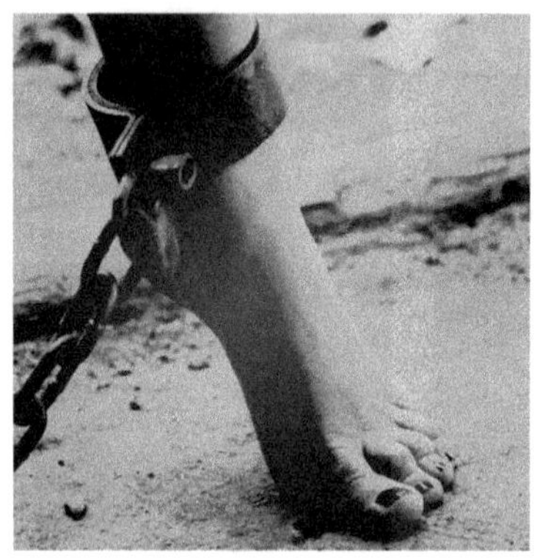

What? Why?
Fists on chest, silence beads company,
Madman returns, agony needs a friend.
The black curls, hands collide,
To untangle the strangled lunacy.
Swallowed by the storm of event,
Ruined life, burnt a lifejacket.
Tainted by shadows of mishaps,
Once disabled, always a cripple,
Merciless was his touch,
Ruthless was his looks,
Stained forever was the young mind,
Paused was her cries,
Fallen sandcastles, shattered ebony,
Still alone in the abyss,
With millions of why,
Why was her mind captive,
Didn't her body feed the gluttony?

BY BLOOD....

Grew up the dynamic duo,
Promised tandem through flow,
Pampered and protected in snow,
Seperations never upset me Joe,
Emotions died inside slow,
Did time invent change,
Or we rode away to land so strange,
Why hide the care,
When you are still there,
We are two of blood,+
Love for you, always in my gut.

LITTLE ONE…

Pink bundle was our prize,
There she was,
Holding our beats in her almond eyes,
Little toes, little nose,
Tiny cries, tiny whines,
Dimple crinkles, joy crinkles,
You filled the empty,
Late to my twenty,
Piece of my heart,
Remains yours when we part,
You are my first lil one,
Holding my heart through every thorn.

JUST FRIENDS….

Walking towards a pipe dream,
I love you said the fool's paradise,
Glassy eyes saw the ripples in stream,
Song on repeat grounded trembling hands,
Played my heart yet here we stand,
Brawny bond, innocent talks,
Overused phrases, same old walks,
Intoxicated waves on shore,
We are dyed friends and no more.

TROPHY...

Exceptional prodigy of proud aristocrats,
Born the epitome of excellence,
Haunted by many treatments,
Unknown was her silence,
She was the talk of the town,
Suppressed was her weekly visits,
Pounding beats and insomnia her nightgown,
Four walls enclosed her secrets,
Broken limbs are aided by crutches,
Broken minds have non absorbable stitches,
Unacceptable was her illness to her aristocrats,
For they can never hold up fragments in their
ads.

FALLEN…

Hope my eternal misery,
Where was hope when I asked for the time left,
Where was hope when my parents cried for one
last time,
Where was hope when I drove everyone from
my life,
Where was hope when I paraded my winnings,
Where was hope when I wanted to breathe a
little,
Where was hope when my lil one wanted me,
Where was hope when I can't fulfill the
promises,
Where is hope when I am still hoping for it?

THREE…

One, two, three,
And you go free,
There was always a glee,
Just at the thought of flee.
Decked at the highest,
When called the finest,
I was crumbled by the honest,
And in three, brought down was my mightiest.
Creeping was a countdown,
While funky dancing through downtown,
Cancer told me I was a disown,
From the very life I was a letdown.

At one there was a knock,
At two for all empathy and shock,
At three I was happy with the talk,
And by eve, I was told to take the walk,
To a distance till time stops on the clock.

THE SINGSONG…

Don't Blame Me for the Love Story,
Can't Shake It Off even in the Wildest Dreams,
I Knew You Were Trouble, but not anymore Lover,
Cause I know All Too Well you are no Taylor
Swift.
Everything I Wanted was just a Bellyache,
Those Ocean Eyes held me Hostage,
Happier Than Ever was I,
But I was just 8 when All The Good Girls Go To
Hell,
And I was broke when Billie Eilish slayed.

The Little Things were Falling again,
The Late Night Talking was One Thing,
To the world You And I were Perfect,
But we never made it to the Best Song Ever like
Harry Styles.
Boy With Love was Yet To Come,
To Make It Right every Spring Day,
Fake Love fired the Dynamite,
I Need You like every soul needs BTS.
Don't take me Back To You,
I don't want the Same Old Love with the Bad Liar,
Just let it Slow Down,
Who Says? People You know,
The Wizard of Waverly Place, Selena Gomez.

THRILLS…

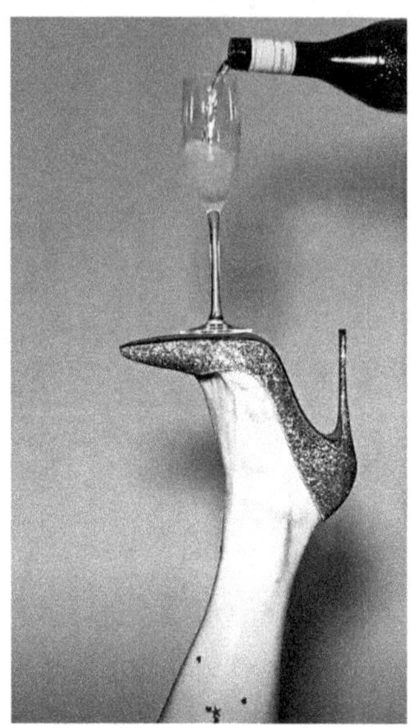

Pretty lies by thrifty girls,
Money spent by honey dudes,
Party nights and holy martinis,
Drunken truth faces broken hearts.

FEETISH…

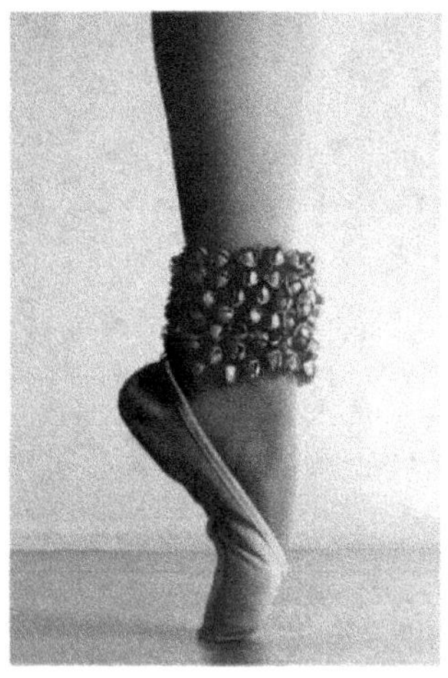

Rain, rays, or any time,
Prime my feet and let's sway,
Play the music, sing no song,
Crown me queen, but buy me shoes.
Tame my body, swing my hands,
Stand on toes, passion sought,
Taught my feet need no earth,
Birth was the sky, had no limit,
Trinket sparkles through cartwheels and popping,
Rocking hiphops and, blooming classical,
Sentinel may be life, yet louder will be my fetish.

ARTIST....

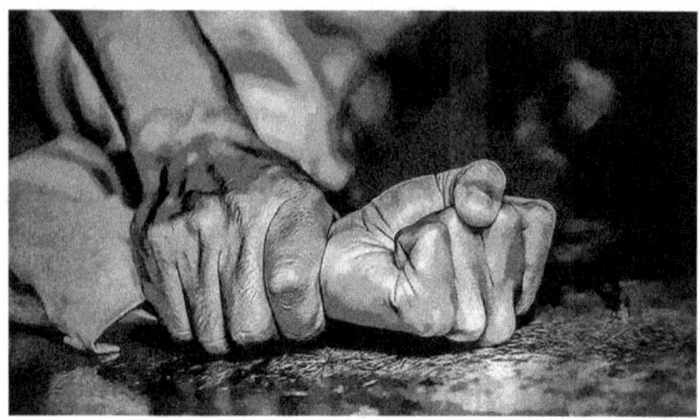

Created solidity, promoted mellow,
Painted for beauty, sold for pressure,
Why are males not taught,
The late night dread of rapes?
Closed doors to intruders,
Opened pleasures to insiders.
Constant fears, repeated cries,
Hide my arms, hide my legs,
Hide my face, hide my body,
Why not hide the felon and strike the sick
thoughts?
2 months, 8 years, 25 years and even 60 years,
Age is just another rapture,
Molest is everyday story,
Rapists are country's artists,
For laws are their rules,
Their sins are talented wins.
Kills at sight of her, pills at thoughts of her.

PARTED…

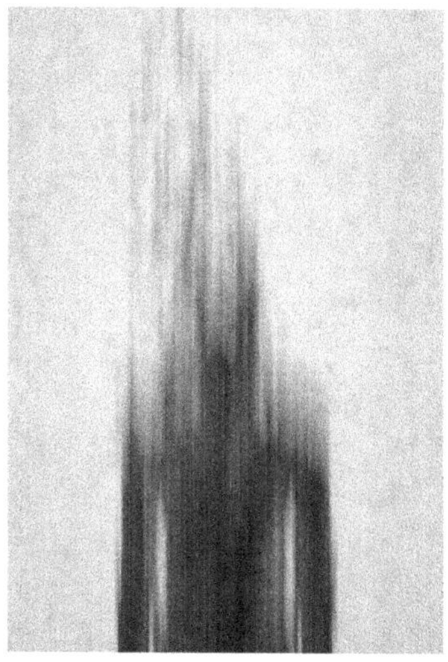

Your dream is our fight,
Your parting is our war,
Your cry is our drive,
Your memory is our color,
You don't live now, yet here you are,
You live in me, breathing in every cell.

STOP ME....

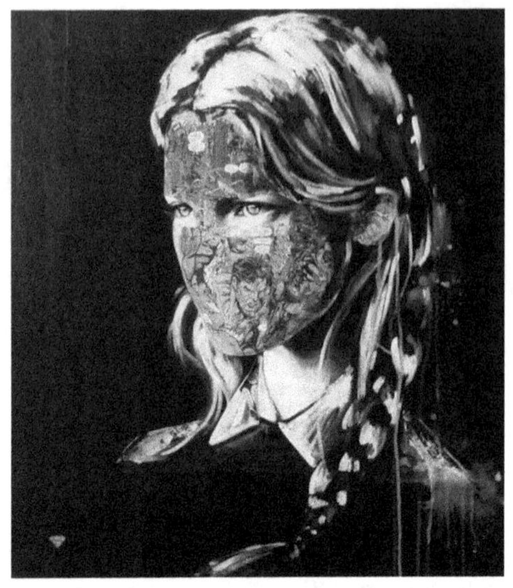

I run, I flex my feminine,
I jump, I bleed every month,
I laugh, I mop watch soaps,
I fly, I chain my dreams,
I win, I crumble through failure,
I fight, I silence my valor,
Do not tame me woman, do not name me man,
I am just another human, just another you.

PIONEER....

Portrays fatherhood.
Portrays strength.
Portrays riches.
Portrays masculinity.
Portrays dominance.
Albeit,
Bonafide he is my buddy,
Bona fide he is my dulcet,
Bona fide he is my modesty,
Bona fide he is my bulwark,
Bona fide he is my stairway.

BFF…

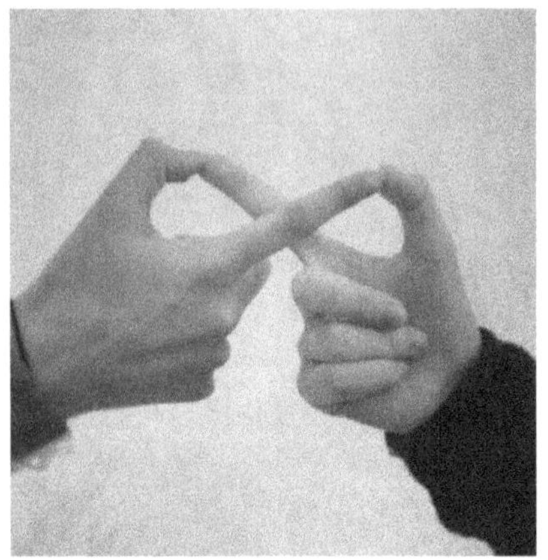

She is the north, I am the south,
She is the sarcasist when I am the subject,
She is the vibe when I am the spirit,
She is the energy when I am the talent,
She is the wall when I am in the fall,
She is the ebony to my ivory,
She is the constant to my every moment.

BUTTERFLY....

Wings unfolded, broken bubbles,
Flutters the tides, broken commands,
Metaphor heals, broken seals,
Flying the odds, broken copies,
Delight the beauty, broken standards,
Embrace darkness, broken norms.

QUESTIONS…

An end? A Beginning?
Shatters of hope? Glitters of love?
Hugs of warmth? Hands of death?
Meet at destiny? Meet at illusion?
Saved from dread? Cut to shreds?
Cloud the questions? Answers bleed honesty?
What if?

SECRETS....

He broke the world for me,
He tore down the norms for me,
He kissed the pain off of me,
He held me in every misery,
He colored my creeping darkness,
He loved my every flaws,
Silently waiting,
Hearts racing,
Until you reveal,
Secrets to the veil.

EXPECTATION....

Deception attracts my friends,
The happy deceives,
The laugh deceives,
The bond deceives.
Commitment is deception,
Would you be a sentimentalist? Or another
fearless?
Blue birds should fly,
Leave alone and not pry,
For if there is a chain, she will not shy,
She will peck you till you die.

MEAN GIRLS....

Walked the hallways,
High heels and red tints,
LV and Dior owned sleeks,
Muted every look of envy,
Insta, Twitter adorned bodies,
Snickers at oily hairs,
Laughs at the price of every nerd,
Allies the hotties,
Lives off scandals,
Infecting aura splits the air,
Fabricated lies,
Jokes aside, they were known dead inside.

LEAP OF FAITH....

Faith, hope, endear,
Words to life.
Created me, created paths,
Holds my hand, holds my mind,
Pivots my fall, pivots my evil,
Wakes my dreams, wakes me to real,
Shows my path, shows my choice,
Leap of faith is my devotion.

FORCED….

It drove me to commit sins,
It pushed me to push them off,
It forced me to break the bond,
Blame game is not what it is,
For amidst the options,
Our choice is to choose the one,
The one not risky, the one very pretty,
For we are more than just humans,
We are mortal yet not our souls.

MIRAGE....

Behold my heir,
Met her in the lair,
Glaring mystic hazel eyes held me captive,
Dressed was she for every festive,
Shuts the world in her satire,
Every envy deemed her backfire,
Played hard to get,
Made me kneel to her in debt,
Screamed survival,
Her life turned critical,
Weird and dramatic were those days,
Sent to a maze at what she says,
Silence spoke leaving void,

She was magnolia, she said,
Fallen yet surrounded,
Not the one to be grounded,
Faraway to her pathway,
Walked around midday,
Stopped and saw a mirage,
There she was an eyeful to watch.

TRAUMA.....

Spiraling the deepest pits,
Hitting the hardest rocks,
I never found the lights.
Groovin the greatest fear,
Reminiscing the monsters,
Shadows pry in every dream,
Even if locked in that white castle,
Eyes don't betray movements,
Flashbacks of despicable acts,
Running away and away,
Into the same dark forest,
Hallucinations and illusions,
It never lets go, everyday, I sigh awoke.

MYSTERY SHOES…

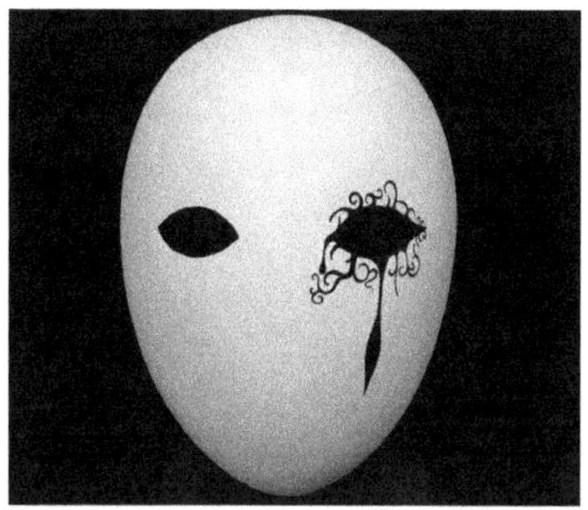

Mystery shoes of yours,
Leaving trails in my fantasy,
Uptight is your style,
Captivated I am to your poet,
You are witty and known,
I am your salient admirer,
Will you ever see my riddle?
Will you fit my puzzle?
Or is this another passing?
Delusion or a chimera?

AMORIST....

No kissing prince, no white horses,
No sleeping beauty, no fitting shoes,
Defined by darks and scars.
Drew my butterflies around my flaws,
Wrote words of wine,
Drunk on them languishly.
Mind is my savior,
Heart is my liar,
One sings and speaks,
Other silent and sorry,
This is my escape.
This is my agape.

www.ingramcontent.com/pod-product-compliance
Lightning Source LLC
LaVergne TN
LVHW051225200726
843510LV00011B/1487